WILDFIRES

SEYMOUR SIMON

SCHOLASTIC INC.
New York Toronto London Auckland Sydney
Mexico City New Delhi Hong Kong

PHOTO CREDITS
Permission to use the following photographs is gratefully acknowledged:
pages 5, 11, 13, Dan Morrison; pages 6–7, 9, 25, 26–27, 30, Seymour Simon;
pages 14–15, 17, 21, 31, Alan and Sandy Carey; pages 19, 23, Gary Braasch/*Life;*
pages 28–29, John J. Lopinot/Silver Image; page 32, Gary Braasch
Front jacket photograph © John J. Lopinot/Silver Image; back jacket photograph © Gary Braasch

ISBN 0-439-08089-4

Published by Scholastic Inc., 555 Broadway, New York, NY 10012,
by arrangement with William Morrow & Company, Inc.

12 11 10 9 8 7 6 5 4 3 2 9/9 0 1 2 3 4/0

Printed in the U.S.A. 14

First Scholastic printing, September 1999

The text type is 18-point Garamond Book.

With love for my grandson Joel
and his new brother, Benjamin

A raging wildfire is a frightening thing. Living trees burn as fast as cardboard boxes in a bonfire. Flames race through the treetops, sometimes faster than a person can run, burning at temperatures hot enough to melt steel. A wildfire can be a major disaster, capable of destroying hundreds of homes and costing human lives.

But not all fires are bad. Fires in nature can help as well as harm. A burned forest allows young plants to begin growing. And fire is necessary for some trees, such as sequoias, to release their seeds. Instead of being an ending, fire is often a new chapter in the continuing story of the natural world.

A fire is a chemical reaction, and it needs three things to burn: fuel, oxygen, and heat. During a fire, energy is released as heat and light, which is why fires are so hot and so bright. When a fire is done, there is nothing left but ash. Ash is the form the fuel takes after the chemical reaction of fire is over.

Fires not only release heat, they are also caused by heat. A fire can be caused by a burning match, a flash of lightning, or a glowing ember in a dying camp fire. Once a fire starts, the heat from the fire can cause other fires to start in nearby materials. A burning leaf can set fire to a nearby

leaf without touching it, just from the intense heat. The flaming leaves can then set fire to a branch, which can set fire to the whole tree. In a short while, a fire can leap to another tree, and then another and another. A whole forest can be set ablaze from a tiny fire no bigger than the flame from a match.

Fires also need oxygen to burn. Oxygen is an invisible gas in the air we breathe. One of the reasons wet wood rarely burns is that the water prevents air from getting to the fire. That's why water is used to fight fires in homes and in forests.

For many years, Smokey the Bear warned that "only you" could prevent forest fires, making people think that all fires were enemies. But wildfires are a fact of life in the wilderness, and plants and animals have adjusted to them. Many trees are so dependent on fires that they need cycles of fire in order to grow. Other kinds of trees and shrubs quickly grow back after a fire, often healthier than before. Animals are rarely killed in forest fires. Most are able to flee from a spreading fire. And plants that grow quickly after a fire provide food for animals that might otherwise starve.

In fact, aggressively fighting fires has probably decreased the number of wildfires that help a forest renew itself while increasing the number of more dangerous fires. Scientists say that by stamping out all fires as soon as they start, people have allowed leaves, dead wood, twigs, and bark to accumulate on the forest floor. This provides much more fuel to feed big wildfires than would be the case if small fires were allowed to burn naturally. A director of the United States Forest Service has said that it is not a question of "whether these areas will burn, but only a question of when."

The summer of 1988 was hot and dry in Yellowstone National Park. Almost no rain fell, less than in any year for the previous hundred years. On June 23, a flash of lightning started a fire near Shoshone Lake in the southwest part of the park. In a few weeks, a total of eight major fires were burning. Six of these fires were caused by lightning and were allowed to burn. The other two fires were caused by human carelessness and were fought from the beginning.

Since 1972, Yellowstone Park officials had allowed fires started by lightning to burn themselves out unless they threatened structures built by people. In the next sixteen years, there had been over two hundred such natural fires. But as the fires and smoke drove tourists from the park in the summer of 1988, officials changed their minds. In mid-July, they ordered fire fighters to attack the Shoshone fire, which was coming close to the park buildings at Grant Village. Finally the officials abandoned their policy of letting lightning fires burn naturally, and they launched what was to become the greatest fire-fighting effort in the history of the United States.

Hundreds of fire fighters were sent to battle the eight major blazes. But by then, more than fifty smaller ones had started, most from new lightning strikes. The old fires continued to spread, while the small fires raced toward one another and merged into even bigger fires. Giant lodgepole pines and spruce firs burst into flames like matchsticks. Boulders and rocks exploded in the heat of the flames.

There was more bad news. On August 19, gale-force winds gusted to sixty miles per hour, blowing hot embers a mile downwind and starting new fires. The winds also whipped the flames forward and fed them oxygen. Some of the fires moved through the trees at speeds of up to five miles per hour, much faster than most forest fires and as fast as a person can run. On August 20, known as Black Saturday, 165,000 acres of forest, an area more than twice the size of the entire city of Chicago, were burning. But the worst was still ahead.

By early September, most of the fires in the park were completely out of control. Thick clouds of bitter black smoke covered the Yellowstone valley. One of the major fires, the North Fork, was racing toward Old Faithful, the famous geyser. The geyser couldn't burn, but the nearby Old Faithful Inn—the world's largest log cabin, and as flammable as a huge tinderbox—was directly in the fire's path.

Weary fire fighters tried to wet down the roof and walls of the inn, but it seemed hopeless. The fire was just too strong. Sparks and glowing embers shot over the cabin and set fire to the trees at the other end of the parking lot. It seemed as if the inn would soon be consumed by flames.

Suddenly, at the last moment, the winds shifted and the fires turned away from Old Faithful. On Saturday, September 10, heavy rains began to drench the area around the inn. The next morning, it snowed. While some fires in the park would continue to burn until November, the worst was over. More than twenty-five thousand fire fighters had been called in to help. They had used more than one hundred fire engines and an equal number of planes and helicopters to drop millions of gallons of water and chemicals to slow the advancing flames. But it was the weather, not human beings, that finally ended that summer of fire.

By the time the fires had all died out, about 800,000 acres inside the park had burned, along with another 600,000 acres in the national forests and other lands nearby. About sixty-five buildings had been destroyed, and two people died in the fires. To many people watching on television, it seemed as if the park had been scorched by the flames and would never recover. But that was not so. Nearly two-thirds of the park had not been touched by fire, and even the one-third that had burned was starting to recover.

The wind-driven fires of 1988 left a mosaic of green and black patches in the forests of Yellowstone. Depending upon the extent of the fires, some places looked like green islands in a sea of black trees, while others looked like black tar on a green carpet.

After a fire, burned areas quickly burst into life. In fact, when the ground is still warm from the fires, ants, wood beetles, millipedes, and centipedes are busy. Fire beetles actually seek out fire to breed and lay their eggs in charred logs. The first plants that appear are those whose roots and seeds were there before the fire. But soon new seeds are carried in by the wind and on the fur of animals or in their droppings.

The green-and-black mosaic favors newly arrived plants and animals. Hawks and owls hunt for food in the opened spaces. Tree-drilling woodpeckers hunt for insects beneath the bark of fallen trees. The dead trees also make good nesting sites; bluebirds and tree swallows move in. The fields of new grasses and wildflowers attract grazing animals, and birds come from all over to catch insects in the meadows.

If you watch the movie *Bambi,* you might think that deer and other animals panic and flee in all directions from rapidly approaching flames. But that is not what really happens. Fires often move slowly through forests and grasslands. Larger animals, such as bears, elk, bison, moose, and deer, simply walk away from the fire. Bison and elk graze as usual, sometimes on the flaming edges of the fire. Elk even step over fiery logs to get at patches of unburned grass. The animals that are affected die mostly from smoke inhalation rather than from the flames.

Fires rarely start during the wet spring breeding season, so nests of fledglings are not usually threatened, and at other times of year mature birds can fly off in advance of a fire. Rodents and other small animals dash away across fields or seek shelter in underground burrows or in rocky places. Bears, coyotes, foxes, hawks, falcons, and ravens feast on animals driven from their burrows or on the bodies of animals killed by the smoke. For these scavengers, fire offers many sources of food. Nature quickly adjusts to changes and finds new life even in death.

The forests of Yellowstone are mostly lodgepole pine trees. Many of the lodgepoles were several hundred years old at the time of the 1988 fire. As a lodgepole ages, it doesn't produce enough resin, or sap, to stop insects from boring into its bark, which eventually kills the tree. In very old lodgepole forests, many of the standing trees are dead. Fire removes these dead trees, making room for new ones.

Fire also helps the lodgepole reproduce. This tree has two kinds of cones. One opens normally, over time, and its winged seeds whirl to the forest floor. That is how lodgepoles usually sprout. The other kind of seed is sealed in a rock-hard pine resin that opens only when the heat of a fire melts and burns away the resin.

Following the Yellowstone fires, seed counts in burned lodgepole stands were very high, ranging from fifty thousand to one million seeds per acre. All had come from sealed pinecones that were opened by the fire. Most of these seeds would be eaten by chipmunks, squirrels, birds, and other small animals, but some seeds would sprout, starting a new cycle of life in the forest.

Just two years after the 1988 fires, burned areas had sprouted new plants of all kinds. The pink flowers of fireweed soon appeared. Asters, lupine, and dozens of other kinds of plants grew among the burned trees. Insects returned in great numbers and began to feast on the plants. In turn, the insects became food for birds and other insect eaters. Elk and bison grazed on the plants. Chipmunks gathered seeds, and small rodents built nests in the grasses.

The young lodgepole pines are now waist high, and many different kinds of plants surround them. Before the fire, the towering older trees blocked sunlight from the forest floor, allowing only a few other species of plants to flourish there. Without periodic fires, low-growing plants that have survived in the park for thousands of years would die off completely.

In fifty to one hundred years, the lodgepoles will again be tall enough to deprive other plant species of the light they need to grow. The forest will become mostly pines. Then the fires are likely to return, and the cycle of burning and rebirth will continue.

These fire fighters are not trying to put out a fire. Instead they started this fire and are letting it burn. Using a device called a drip torch, fire fighters set small blazes on purpose to prevent large-scale forest fires by burning away undergrowth and dead wood in Kings Canyon, California.

Many forests and grasslands in North America are dependent on fire to thin out old, dying trees and other plants. For many years, the main focus of fire prevention has been to put out natural fires as soon as possible, but the longer the fuel builds up in a forest, the worse the fire is going to be—and the more likely it will be to burn out of control. So fire is now actually being put to use. Florida, for example, burns more than a million acres of grasslands a year. In that state, the new slogan is "Using fires wisely prevents forest fires."

Everglades National Park is part of a vast sea of saw grass that covers four thousand square miles in southern Florida. The "glades" are home for many wading birds, as well as for turtles and alligators. During the summer's rainy season, saw-grass fires often start because of lightning. The fires burn the parts of the plant above the water, and the ashes provide minerals for new growth. Without periodic fires, the saw grass would age, die, and decay, filling up the swamps. The Everglades need fires in order to survive. Lightning fires in the glades are permitted to burn except during droughts. Fire crews also burn saw grass along the park boundaries, thus preventing larger fires in dry years.

Eight years after the fires of 1988, Yellowstone is still renewing itself. Burned trees are losing their blackened bark and turning a silvery gray. Meadows are growing around them. The burned areas are slowly fading away.

Meanwhile scientists still have a lot to learn about what happens to a forest after a huge fire. One question they ask: How often does an area burn naturally?

The time between natural fires varies, depending upon climate and tree life. In Yellowstone's lodgepole pine forests, the interval between large natural fires is three hundred to four hundred years. In Florida's slash pines, the interval is only seven years, and it is as short as two to five years in the open ponderosa forests of northern Arizona. In the cedar-spruce forests of western Washington State, two thousand years can pass between fires!

Wildfires are neither good nor bad. In forests and grasslands, they are part of the endless cycle of change.